From #EndSARS to #RegionalGovt:

The Youth-Led Movement for Change"

By

Victor Alade

ISBN: 978-978-58940-2-8

“The destiny of a nation is in the hands of its young people. The tyranny of an extractive leadership will not afford you any ready opportunity for change but you must take it anyway. With force of determination, wilfulness, responsibility and courage, change comes.”

Foreword

As an Investigative Journalist and scholar of African Political studies, I have had the privilege of studying and analysing the political landscape of various countries across the African continent. It's important to note that Nigeria has always held a special place due to its strategic importance in the continent, its abundant resources and its vibrant and diverse population. My research work on Liberia and Sierra Leone Civil Wars gave me a better appreciation of the strategic influence of Nigeria on other countries in Africa.

Nigeria's journey to democracy has been a tumultuous one, with many challenges and setbacks along the way. Despite these challenges, the country has made significant progress over the years, particularly in the area of democratic governance. However, the #ENDSARS protests across the country in 2020 remain another turn point in the political history of the country. The emergence of the #Obidient movement which some Political watchers see as by-product of #ENDSARS clearly shows Nigeria is evolving politically with positive hope for the future.

This book, "From #EndSARS to #RegionalGovt: The Youth-Led Movement for Change" by Victor Alade is a timely and important contribution to the on-going conversation about Nigeria's political development. It chronicles the journey of a group of young Nigerians who, through their tireless activism and advocacy, have captured the attention of the nation and brought to the forefront critical issues that must be addressed.

The book provides a detailed analysis of the #EndSARS movement and the subsequent emergence of the #Obidient movement, highlighting the challenges faced by the youth of Nigeria and the urgent need for change. It makes a compelling case for the adoption of a regional system of government, providing a thorough examination of the benefits of such a system and how it can help to address some of the longstanding issues facing Nigeria.

I am particularly impressed by the way in which the book places the voices and experiences of young Nigerians at the centre of the conversation. It is a powerful testament to the resilience, creativity, and determination of Nigeria's youth, and a reminder that they are the key to the country's future.

As Nigeria moves forward under a new president, it is essential that young people continue to play an active role in the political process and engage incoming administration constructively. This book will serve as a valuable resource for anyone who seeks to understand the challenges facing Nigeria and the potential solutions that can help to address them. It is my hope that this book will inspire young people to continue to demand accountability, transparency, and good governance from their leaders, and to work towards building a brighter future for Nigeria.

In conclusion, I commend the author for his dedication and commitment to this important cause. I believe that this book will serve as a catalyst for change and an inspiration to all those who seek a better future for Nigeria.

-Oyewale Oyelola
Managing Editor, FactualTimes

Introduction

Nigeria has had a long history of struggles for democracy and good governance. And since the coming of Twitter, the nation has had more trending hashtags on political development to have even warranted a ban at some point. The most recent of these struggles is the #EndSARS protest, which shook the nation in October 2020. The protests, which started as a peaceful demand for the disbandment of the Special Anti-Robbery Squad (SARS), quickly spiralled into a nationwide movement against police brutality, corruption, and bad governance. The youth, who are the majority of Nigeria's population, played a pivotal role in the #EndSARS protest, and their voices were heard loud and clear.

The #EndSARS movement will go down in history as a turning point in the country's democracy. The movement, which was largely driven by the youth, was not only a protest against police brutality but also lack of accountability of the government. The protests saw thousands of young people take to the streets to demand an end to police brutality and bad governance. Despite the peaceful nature of the protests, it was met with excessive force by the government which led to several deaths and injuries. Apparently, the government had never envisaged that young people could come together to propagate such a brooding nationwide protests at the time and they did quite know the best way to respond in quelling it without violence.

Following the EndSARS protest, many young Nigerians came to the realization that they could no longer leave the future of the country in the hands of the older generation. This realization led to the birth of the #Obidient movement, a political movement that seeks to give young Nigerians a voice in the political space. Just like an artist who finds his muse in a poet, the youth seem to have found their inspiration from a former Governor of Anambra State; Peter Obi in whose name the 'Obedient' was born. The man himself was not in any way misaligned from the political hegemonies of the country, although he was so painted to the electorate. In any case, the youth saw in him the ideal candidate, relatively young and having credence to their yearnings of good governance. Indeed, it has been long way coming, this yearning and clamour for leadership in the country. Nigeria is believed to be aback footed because of lack of good characters in its political leadership. This leadership gap has become a more prominent concern since just after the 4th republic. It has become increasingly noticeable that the political class only continued to protect and advance their own self-interests in every way, leaving the citizens to toil under their wasteful, exclusive grasp of the polity.

So, having experienced so much neglect over the last 20 years or more, young people have grown a high level of awareness and intolerance to misrule of the political class. Thus, the movement is anchored on the belief that the youth can no longer afford to be bystanders in the political process but must be actively involved in shaping the future of the country.

However, the EndSARS movement, which without doubt rattled the government, was just the beginning of a new era in Nigeria. The youth, who make up over 60% of the population, have realized the power they hold and are determined to use it to effect change in the country. They waited till the 2023 general elections. But before then, both the incumbent party and the main opposition laboriously tried to play down the growing influence of the Obidient movement. They labelled the movement a party with no political structures and vilified them vigorously to the extent of becoming profusely adamant that they posed any threat at the polls. But the government in power and the main opposition knew that the movement will upset their individual chances, only that they chose to downplay the effects by not admitting it.

At the Presidential election, this young people-led, 'structure-less' party, #Obidient Movement, put up a strong showing at the polls where its presidential candidate garnered over 6 million votes, coming in no distant third in the contest as the other two parties had maliciously foretold. For a party who only relied on young people for structures, many didn't believe they could win such huge number of votes.

The presidential election was keenly contested and won by the incumbent party, the All Progressives Congress, APC. Although the election has been adjudged to be credible and fair but many section of the electorate, especially the opposition and of course #Obidient Movement, believe the electoral body has performed below expectation. Few days after the election, its Presidential candidate decided to challenge the victory of the incumbent party at the election tribunals.

It is noteworthy to mention that, leading to the polls; ethnic divisions were noticeably a factor in deciding the winner. Ethno-religious sentiments and drums of ethnic preservation were sounded to the loudest. Almost at no times past was Nigeria become more divided nor the nation's electoral pivot gruesomely blunted by infractions of ethnic cooperation that had previously existed.

Before the election, there had been calls for self-determination by virtually all major ethnic groups in the country. While it was somewhat a benign course in the southwest with the Yoruba Nation agitators, somewhere else in the Southeastern part of the country it has always been fatal.

Notwithstanding the winner of the Presidential election, the call for self-determination may likely resurge. And really it should be expected. It wouldn't have mattered even if the main opposition or the #Obidient candidate had won the election; the people are already on the precipice of making the decision that advances regional interests rather than a unitary one and they don't seem to relent from pursuing the idea even further. However, rather than full blown breaking away, it is believed in the quarters of many well-meaning Nigerians that constitutional restructuring could be the solution to the reoccurring ethno-religious crisis in the country. These crises which are often created by lopsided advantages and competition on State's resources allocation control, population density vis-à-vis number of Local Government areas and States created in various regions of the country. These are factors, out of many that outsets the challenges which characterize the divisions that brew during every Nigeria's presidential elections as we witnessed in 2023.

Many have argued that the presidential system of government that we run is not sustainable for a diverse country like Nigeria with over 250 ethnic groups. Since the 4th republic, the Central government had failed to show that they have genuine plans to restructure the country in a way to take care of these concerns. Although there had been previous effort to come with referendums and committees on restructuring within the last 15 years, however, the government has never implemented the reports of the committees. The failure of government after government in this regard has continued to amplify the voice of people from different ethnic regions of the country who share the sentiments of self-determination.

Personally, I agree that a regional government would be a solution for Nigeria's political problems rather than the breaking away of the country to different parts. Regional government will solve the problem of resource control to the states because in the case, the federal government, headed by a prime minister will only oversee the administration of regional heads with minimal interference.

This book is a call to action for the Nigerian youth one more time. It is now time for the youth of Nigeria to redirect this energy towards a new cause - the demand for a regional government. It is a call for young people to sustain the energy and momentum that was generated by the #EndSARS and #Obidient movements and redirect it towards demanding for a regional system of government in Nigeria. A regional government will not only give more power to the states but will also address the ethnic and religious biases that inflame the divisions amongst us as citizens.

In this book, we will explore the concept of regional government, its benefits, and how it can be implemented in Nigeria. We will also examine the challenges that must be overcome to make regional government a reality in Nigeria. One of the aims of this book is to educate young Nigerians about the concept of regional government and how it can be used as a tool for good governance that they have been yearning for. The regional system of government is a concept that has been in existence in Nigeria in the past and has the potential to provide a solution to the many challenges facing the country.

Chapter One

Delving into a bit of History and Perspectives of Government

In a country as diverse as Nigeria, it is important to recognize and promote the diversity of cultures and languages. Regional government allows for the development of regional identities and promotes the development of regions based on their unique strengths. Thus, it is a type of governance structure that promotes cultural diversity and regional development.

In this chapter, you will also be introduced to the concept of regional government and how it differs from the current presidential system of government in Nigeria. You will be accustomed to the benefits of regional government, such as increased citizen participation in governance, resource control, and economic development. Unlike the extractive political institution currently in operation in the country where power resides in a few, regional government promote inclusivity in the structures within each regions of the country.

Our nation's economic fate is not determined by geography or culture or even religion as the politicians under the Presidential system has discolored it. Rather, the failure of our government, economically speaking, is manmade, and not geography or religion that determine the prosperity of our country. Though ethno-religious intolerance has been one of the debilitating challenges to

Nigeria's development after corruption, the cause of the former can be attributed to the latter. As we have seen in the Nigeria example, the presidential system and corruption are siamese twins. Since the 1st republic, all Nigeria's Heads of government have been involved in one corruption scandal or the other which have contributed to the collapse of the country to a state of dire infrastructures or no working institution.

The presidential system of government we practice in this clime is of even grave extractive nature. The engendering corruption of the system has always been the bane of Nigeria's growth and development. What was held as cherished national values has been eroded by the extractive political and economic institutions of the country. I am trying to let you see that this unfortunate phenomenon of corruption is not a recent bride that the political class in Nigeria is trying to tame; it is the favourite one that the presidential system has always been beloved with. The system handed the affairs of our nation in those who favour private gains over public benefits right from the time of the amalgamation of the Northern and Southern Protectorate of Nigeria. Regrettably, it has become obvious that the only notable surviving legacy of the successive political leadership, both civilian and military, that has managed the affairs of the country at different times since then has been the institutionalisation of corruption in all agencies of the public service. And with a hand of friendship extended to capitalist friends and allies in the private sectors, corruption like a deadly virus, has subsequently crumbled the fabrics of the Nigerian economy.

But the new generation of Nigerians will not continue to allow this maladministration of government at all levels to continue, or so it appears. With the advantage of technology that provided access to information to young people in the country, their voices are becoming increasingly amplified in demanding for true change.

Power cannot remain concentrated in the hands of a few people. As Daron Acemoglu and James A. Robinson argued in *'Why Nations Fail?',* "Where Political power has been narrowly concentrated, and has been used to create wealth for those who possess it, there is bound to be poverty."

Since the 4th republic, power at the centre has always rotated between the two major political parties in the country, the PDP and the APC which has had change of nomenclature and affiliations over the years. The PDP, while in government became so emboldened by their grip on the nation that it had even boasted to remain in power for 60 years.

Shortly after this declaration, in 2015, the APC unseated the PDP in the presidential election, the first time an incumbent party was defeated in the country. The defeat of the PDP and the victory of

APC then was a protest demonstration of dissatisfaction of citizens in the failure of the government. They wanted a change, just like the #Obidient movement almost changed the Change in February, 2023. As it appears, the movement invariably started in 2015, resurfaced in 2023 and will most probably come back in 2027 until government demonstrate an inclusivity that promotes the development of citizens, especially young people who occupy the highest population in the country.

Citizens of countries that Nigeria disingenuously pattern its government after, such as Britain and United States have in the times past overthrew the elites who controlled power and created a society where political rights were much more broadly distributed, where the government was accountable and responsive to citizens, and where the great mass of the people could take advantage of economic opportunities. This sort of accountability that is derived from a decentralized government is what makes those countries prosperous. The reverse case of unaccountability in the presidential government of Nigeria goes to show that there is a relationship between poverty and its typical politics. The fact is the presidential form of government harbors people who seem to be benefitting from poverty in Nigeria. These elites, supported by some others in their political enclaves, will always argue that restructuring is not the solution to Nigeria's problem. They garb themselves in garments of nationalism, but in reality, they do not want fundamental changes or reforms. The only things they are willing to change are trivial and cosmetic things like Democracy Day and political party affiliations when and if it doesn't serve their interest any longer. The only sectors of the citizenry that can truly demand the change that is needed are the masses, and the young people have taken the responsibility without going back.

Chapter 2:

Nigeria's Political Challenges and History of Constitutional Democracy"

Let us examine Nigeria's political challenges and how they have impacted the country's development. We look at the role of ethnicity and religion in Nigerian politics, and how these factors have contributed to the country's political instability. Nigeria has faced significant political challenges since its independence in 1960. Ethnic and religious divisions have played a significant role in Nigerian politics, with politicians often exploiting these divisions to gain power. This has led to political instability, corruption, and underdevelopment in the country. Nigeria's current presidential system of government has not been able to effectively address these challenges, and there is a need for a new approach. In this chapter, you will explore how a regional government can address Nigeria's political challenges, and bring about the much-needed change the country needs.

Countries like Germany, Spain, and Canada have been running successful regional governments which Nigeria can take a cue from. These governments have been able to promote economic development, political stability, and citizen participation. They have also been able to resolve issues of resource control and ethnic tensions. Nigeria must learn from their examples and consider the possibility of a regional government system. Nigeria has been grappling with issues of resource control and ethnic tensions for many years. The recent calls for secession by some ethnic groups underscored the need for a more inclusive system of government. Learning from successful examples in other countries can help Nigeria find a way forward.

"Exploring Nigeria's History of Constitutional Democracy"

It is important to note that Nigeria is a country with a complex and diverse history, and any analysis of its past governance systems must take into account the perspectives of all regions and ethnic groups. Nonetheless, I will do my best to provide a comprehensive overview of the pre-amalgamation governance systems and their impact on Nigeria's political and economic landscape. We will also look at Nigeria's history of constitutional democracy, and explore how past political systems have shaped the current state of affairs in the country. We will examine the successes and failures of past governments, and highlight how a regional government system could build upon the strengths of previous systems, while avoiding their shortcomings.

Nigeria has experienced several different forms of government since gaining independence in 1960, including military rule, parliamentary democracy, and presidential democracy. Each system has had its strengths and weaknesses, and Nigeria's current system of federalism has faced its fair share of challenges. Nigeria's political system has evolved over time and at every point, ethnic and religious divisions have played a role in shaping the country's political landscape. Ethnic and religious divisions have played a significant role in Nigeria's political landscape. The country is home to over 250 ethnic groups, each with its own unique culture and identity. These ethnic divisions have often led to conflicts and tensions, particularly during election cycles. Nigeria's political system has also been shaped by its colonial history and the struggles for independence. The country has had several constitutions, including the 1960 Constitution, the 1963 Constitution, the 1979 Constitution, and the 1999 Constitution. Each of these constitutions attempted to address the challenges facing the country at the time, but none has been able to provide a lasting solution to the country's political problems. Despite these challenges, Nigeria has made significant progress in recent years, including the peaceful transfer of power from one democratic government to another. However, there is still a long way to go in terms of addressing corruption, promoting transparency, and ensuring that all Nigerians have a voice in the political process. We will explore how regional government could help address these issues.

First, let's see a bit of history of Regional Government in Nigeria. Has it been practiced before or not, and if so, why abandon it? The history of regional government in Nigeria can be traced back to the colonial era. Then, the country was divided into three regions, namely Northern, Western, and Eastern regions, each with its own regional government. After independence in 1960, the country retained the regional system of government, which lasted until the military coup of 1966.

The regional government system was reintroduced during the Second Republic, with the country divided into 19 states and one federal capital territory. The regional government system was abolished again during the military regime of Ibrahim Babangida in 1987, and Nigeria has since been governed by a centralized system of government.

Prior to the amalgamation of the Northern and Southern Protectorates in 1914, Nigeria was made up of several distinct regions, each with its own system of governance. The North was governed by a series of emirates, with the Emir serving as the overall leader. The South, on the other hand, was divided into the Western and Eastern regions, each with its own legislative council and executive council. The Western Region had a parliamentary system, while the Eastern Region had a system of indirect rule, in which traditional rulers served as intermediaries between the colonial government and the people. One of the benefits of this system was that it allowed for a degree of autonomy and self-determination within each region. For example, the Western

Region was known for its progressive policies, including free education and healthcare, which helped to promote economic growth and social development. Similarly, the Eastern Region's emphasis on indirect rule helped to preserve local traditions and customs while still allowing for modernization and development.

However, there were also some downsides to this system. One of the biggest challenges was the lack of coordination and communication between the different regions, which often led to conflict and competition for resources. For example, the Northern Emirs were often seen as resistant to modernization and are less willing to work with the colonial government than their counterparts in the South.

The amalgamation of the Northern and Southern Protectorates in 1914 was intended to address some of these challenges and create a more unified and cohesive country. However, it also had some unintended consequences. One of the most significant was the creation of a centralized system of government that gave more power to the federal government at the expense of the regions. This led to a loss of autonomy and self-determination, as well as a greater focus on national politics at the expense of regional development.

Economically, Nigeria was more prosperous before the amalgamation, as each region was able to focus on its own strengths and resources. The Western Region, for example, was known for its cocoa production, while the Eastern Region was known for its palm oil. This allowed each region to develop its own unique economy and infrastructure, which contributed to overall economic growth and development.

However, the extractive nature of Nigeria's government after the amalgamation can be traced back to several factors, including the concentration of power at the federal level and the legacy of colonialism. The federal government became increasingly focused on extracting resources from the regions to support national development, which led to a neglect of local infrastructure and development. This created a sense of resentment among many Nigerians, particularly those in the South who felt that their resources were being exploited for the benefit of the North.

Overall, there are certainly benefits and drawbacks to both the pre-amalgamation and post-amalgamation governance systems in Nigeria. The key is to find a system that balances the need for national unity and coordination with the need for regional autonomy and self-determination. A regional system of government, as we are advocating for, could potentially achieve this balance by allowing for greater regional control over resources and development while still maintaining a strong federal government to oversee national issues and policies.

Chapter 3

Arresting the drawbacks

Firstly, it is important to emphasize that a regional system of government does not mean complete independence and isolation of regions. Rather, it is about finding a balance between the need for national unity and coordination, and the need for regional autonomy and self-determination. With this in mind, some strategic solutions to promote effective regional governance in Nigeria include:

Establishing a system of cooperative federalism: In this system, the central government works in partnership with the regional governments to identify shared goals and priorities, and to allocate resources accordingly. This approach has been successful in countries such as the United States, where the federal government and state governments work together to promote national goals such as economic development, while also respecting the unique needs and perspectives of individual states.

Encouraging regional self-determination: To promote effective regional governance, it is important to empower the regions to make decisions that affect their own development. This could involve devolving more powers to the regional governments, including the ability to collect and manage their own revenues, and to make decisions about their own economic development and social programs. By giving regions greater autonomy, they are able to develop policies and programs that are tailored to their specific needs, and to take responsibility for their own successes and failures.

Creating regional councils: Regional councils can serve as a forum for dialogue and coordination between the different regional governments. They can be composed of representatives from each regional government, as well as representatives from civil society, business, and other sectors. The councils can be responsible for coordinating regional policies and programs, identifying areas of shared interest, and sharing best practices.

Promoting inter-regional collaboration: In addition to cooperation between the central government and the regions, it is important to encourage collaboration between the regions themselves. This can be achieved through initiatives such as joint development projects, shared infrastructure and resources, and the exchange of best practices. Inter-regional collaboration can help to break down barriers between regions, promote greater understanding and cooperation, and create a stronger sense of national unity.

Building capacity at the regional level: To ensure that regional governments are able to effectively manage their own affairs, it is important to build capacity at the regional level. This could involve providing training and resources to regional government officials, and investing in infrastructure and administrative systems that support effective regional governance.

Drawing on the experiences of countries such as the United States and the United Kingdom, there are several key lessons that Nigeria can learn in order to promote effective regional governance. One important lesson is the need for a balance between centralization and decentralization. While a strong central government is important for maintaining national unity and coordination, it is equally important to empower regions to make decisions that affect their own development. Another important lesson is the need for effective mechanisms for dialogue and coordination between the central government and regional governments. By establishing a system of cooperative federalism, Nigeria can ensure that all levels of government are working towards shared goals and priorities.

In conclusion, the establishment of a regional system of government in Nigeria has the potential to promote greater unity, development, and self-determination for all Nigerians. However, to make this system work effectively, it is important to address the challenges of coordination and communication between the different regions. By promoting a balance between centralization and decentralization, empowering regions to make decisions that affect their own development, and establishing effective mechanisms for dialogue and coordination, Nigeria can build a more inclusive, equitable, and prosperous society. Young people can play a crucial role in advocating for this type of governance system and ensuring that it is implemented in a legal, non-violent approach.

That is why in my own opinion, it is important to educate young Nigerians on the country's complex and diverse history of governance, which is one of the main aims of writing this book and to encourage them to think critically about the benefits and drawbacks of different systems. By promoting a legal and non-violent approach to advocacy and activism, young people can help to shape the future of governance in Nigeria and work towards a more inclusive and equitable society. A regional system of government, if implemented properly and with the input and participation of all regions and ethnic groups, has the potential to promote greater unity, development, and self-determination for all Nigerians.

Chapter 4:
Understanding Regional Government

Hello again and thank you for sharing my thoughts on this concept of what I call a sustainable approach to governance in Nigeria if truly we are to achieve unity and progress. I am sure you find it interesting for you to have this book up to this stage. You man probably be wondering what this concept of government really is or perhaps you are thinking about its applicability solving Nigeria's current political challenges. Either way, as citizens, we will have to begin the conversation one way or another and so, we must understand what the concept is all about, think it through before we start to engage the polity and demand for a change. So, this book will provide the necessary education and also inspire you to see the possibilities and run with it.

In this chapter, you will explore the benefits of a regional government system for Nigeria, and how it can address the country's political challenges. Nigeria is a diverse country with over 250 ethnic groups, and the current presidential system of government has not been able to effectively address the country's political challenges. I will also draw your attention to the reasons why a regional government is a potential solution for Nigeria's political challenges, and how it can benefit the country. So I urge you to read the book to the end, and let's explore the world of regional government together.

Regional government is a system of government where power is devolved to regional or state authorities. In this system, the central government shares power with the regional or state authorities who are responsible for making and implementing policies that affect their region. It is a form of decentralized government, where power is not concentrated in the hands of the central government but shared with the regions or states.

The benefits of regional government are numerous. One of the main benefits is that it promotes local participation and accountability. Regional governments are closer to the people and can respond to their needs more effectively than a centralized government. It also allows for more efficient management of resources, as regions can manage their resources according to their needs.

As we have seen, the just concluded presidential election highlighted the need for a more inclusive system of government. Ethnic and religious tensions were major factors in the elections, and there were accusations of vote rigging and other forms of electoral malpractice. These are issues that underscore the need for a more accountable and transparent system of government.

The Need for Regional Government in Nigeria

Let us take a broad look at Nigeria's political landscape and the challenges facing the country. Nigeria is a diverse nation with over 250 ethnic groups, and it has a long history of political instability and corruption. The current system of federal government has not been able to effectively address these challenges, leading to calls for a new approach to governance.

One solution that has been proposed is regional government, where power and resources are decentralized and shared among regions. This system has the potential to promote greater accountability and development at the local level, while also promoting unity and cooperation among regions. We will delve into these benefits and more, later in the book.

Here I want to try and explain how regional government differs from the current presidential system of government. I will also try to discuss the historical background of Nigeria's political system, highlighting the challenges faced by the country in achieving true democracy and finally explore how a regional government could address some of these challenges, including issues of representation and resource control.

Nigeria has a complex history when it comes to constitutional democracy. The country gained independence from Britain in 1960 and since then has struggled to establish a stable democracy. The country has had several constitutions, including the 1960 Constitution, the 1963 Constitution, the 1979 Constitution, and the 1999 Constitution, among others. Each of these constitutions attempted to address the challenges facing the country at the time, but none has been able to provide a lasting solution to the country's political problems.

A regional government could be a solution to some of Nigeria's political problems. A regional government would decentralize power and give more autonomy to the states, which could help to address issues of representation and resource control. By reducing the power of the federal government, a regional government would also help to reduce corruption and improve governance at the state level. As you are already aware, regional government gives room for power to be shared between the central government and regional governments. In this system, the regions have significant autonomy, and are responsible for making decisions on issues such as education, health, and infrastructure. The central government is responsible for issues such as defense, that is, national security and foreign affairs. Regional governments have a greater understanding of the needs of their communities, and are better able to address them. This is why a regional government can lead to better governance and development in Nigeria.

Chapter 5

Far from the Vision

I think it will offer some balance if we could point out the challenges of the current presidential government of Nigeria including corruption, expensive political institution and patronage, low productivity of the civil service and weak political and economic institution, weak judiciary systems and distrust of citizens in their government amongst others. Looking at where the county stands now, I want to be able to show you comparison of the relative importance of what Nigeria has now and what it stands to gain with regional government. This should open the eyes of young people to the rots and inspire them to own the clamour for a more beneficial regional government that is being suggested in this book.

As a large, diverse and resource-rich nation, Nigeria has tremendous potential to be one of the most prosperous and powerful countries in the world. However, the current state of affairs is far from this vision. The current presidential government of Nigeria is plagued by corruption, expensive political institutions and patronage, low productivity of the civil service, weak political and economic institutions, a weak judiciary system, and a general lack of trust from citizens towards their government. These issues have led to a feeling of disillusionment amongst the people of Nigeria, who feel let down by their leaders and yearn for a change. One of the most pressing issues facing Nigeria today is corruption. It is widely acknowledged that corruption is endemic in Nigeria and has seeped into all aspects of public life. From the highest levels of government to the lowest, corruption is seen as a way of life. This has had a devastating effect on the country, sapping its resources, undermining its institutions and depriving its people of the basic services they need to survive.

Another issue facing Nigeria is the high cost of political institutions and patronage. The cost of running the presidential system of government in Nigeria is astronomical and the patronage system that accompanies it only serves to further enrich the political elite at the expense of the masses.

Furthermore, the civil service in Nigeria is notoriously inefficient and unproductive. It is widely acknowledged that many civil servants are unqualified, untrained and uncommitted to their work. This has led to a situation where government services are often sub-standard and unresponsive to the needs of the people.

Weak political and economic institutions are also a major problem facing Nigeria. The country's political parties lack strong ideological foundations and are often driven by personalities rather than policies. This has led to a situation where political parties are often in disarray and unable to deliver on their promises.

In addition, Nigeria's judiciary system is weak and has been undermined by corruption and political interference. This has led to a situation where justice is often delayed or denied, and the rule of law is often flouted.

All of these issues are symptoms of a broader malaise in Nigeria's political system. The current system of government is simply not working for the people of Nigeria. There is a need for a new approach that can address these issues and deliver the kind of change that the country needs.

This is where the idea of regional government comes in. By giving more power and autonomy to the regions, regional government can create a more responsive, accountable and efficient system of government that is better able to meet the needs of the people.

Regional government can provide a more inclusive and decentralized structure for Nigeria. By decentralizing power, the regions will have more control over their own affairs, and this will lead to a greater sense of ownership and responsibility among the people. This will also help to reduce the concentration of power in the hands of a few elites and prevent the kind of patronage system that is so prevalent in Nigeria today.

Regional government can also provide a more efficient system of government. By giving more power to the regions, the central government can focus on the key areas that require its attention, such as foreign policy, national security and economic development. The regions will be better able to manage their own affairs, and this will lead to greater efficiency and productivity in the civil service.

In addition, regional government can help to strengthen Nigeria's political and economic institutions. By giving more power to the regions, there will be a greater sense of competition between them, and this will help to stimulate economic growth and development. The regions will also be better able to develop their own policies and strategies, and this will lead to greater innovation and creativity in the political and economic spheres.

The Presidential system has not really been able to give Nigeria's judiciary system its pride of place. Our judiciary system has been greatly weakened by the influence of a larger-than-life presidential system that is led by the whims and caprices or the body language of the President, and working to the interests of the executives most times. The government selects the Court Order it wants to obey under the current dispensation in Nigeria. A classic example of disobedience to court order was the Supreme Court judgement against Naira redesign policy of the Central Bank of Nigeria just before the elections. The CBN refused to obey the court injunction on the premise of some sort of support from the Presidency. Safe for some recent reforms by the legislative arm of the government on autonomy, the judiciary has remained totally dependent on the executive. Even with the reforms, the judiciary still relied on the executive for their fiscal budget and allocation. So, in the real sense, what the Judiciary had is a quasi-autonomy which is not enough to be independent. I believe that decentralizing power to the regions will provide greater opportunities for the judiciary to operate more effectively and independently. Under the current centralized system, the judiciary is often subject to political interference and corruption, leading to a lack of trust and accountability.

With regional autonomy, there would be greater opportunities for the judiciary to be more responsive to the needs of the people and to uphold the rule of law without fear of political reprisal. Regional governments would have greater control over the appointment and management of judges, ensuring that they are selected based on merit and that they operate independently.

Additionally, regional governments would be better able to provide resources and support to the judiciary, ensuring that it has the capacity to operate effectively and efficiently. This would help to address some of the systemic issues facing the judiciary, such as delays in the resolution of cases and the lack of resources for court operations.

The judicial system in Nigeria under the current system has often been criticized for being too slow, ineffective, and corrupt. The system is often manipulated by politicians, and court decisions can be influenced by bribery or political interference. This has led to a lack of trust in the judiciary system and a failure to hold those in power accountable for their actions. Under a regional system of government, there would be a greater opportunity to strengthen the judiciary system, allowing for greater accountability and a stronger rule of law.

Overall, a regional system of government can provide the necessary framework to strengthen Nigeria's judiciary system and ensure that it operates independently and effectively. By giving more power to the regions, the judiciary will be better able to serve the needs of the people and promote the rule of law.

Finally, there is a significant level of distrust between citizens and the government in Nigeria. This lack of trust is a major obstacle to progress and development, as it hampers cooperation and effective policy implementation. Under a regional system of government, there would be greater opportunities for citizens to engage with their government and have their voices heard. This increased participation and engagement would lead to greater trust in government and a greater willingness to work together for the common good.

Nigeria is facing significant challenges under its current presidential system of government. We have identified these challenges to include corruption, expensive political institutions and patronage, low productivity of the civil service, weak political and economic institutions, weak judiciary systems, and distrust of citizens in the government. A regional system of government could help to address these challenges by creating a more inclusive and decentralized structure that better reflects the needs and desires of the people of Nigeria. Through greater regional autonomy and self-determination, there would be a greater opportunity for economic and political development, greater accountability and transparency, and greater trust between citizens and their government. The time has come for young Nigerians to take up the mantle of change and demand a regional system of government that will empower them to create a brighter future for themselves and for their country.

Chapter 6

The Challenges of Resource Control in Nigeria

The challenges of resource control in Nigeria could be traced to the divisionary problems that plague our national unity. The current system of government has led to a concentration of power and resources at the federal level, which has contributed to economic inequality and underdevelopment in many regions. Regional government system can address these challenges by giving states more control over their resources and promoting local economic development. This book sets to achieve the purpose of calling for a more equitable system of resource control in Nigeria. Calls for restructuring and resource control have been on the rise in Nigeria in recent years. The current system of government has been criticized for favouring some regions over others and promoting economic inequality. For example, Nigeria has always depended on crude oil from the South-South region of the country for his revenue and budgetary allocations have always been benchmarked on crude sales. The nation has been run with oil since February 1958 when Nigeria exported its first crude oil from Oloibiri oil field in Bayelsa State. Since then, crude oil has been the mainstay of Nigeria's economy until very recent times when diversification from oil is being given attention. But then, the Central Government harnessed this resource without a commensurate investment in both physical and social infrastructure of the host communities. The issue of derivations that goes to the oil producing States and its efficient utilization is a topic for another day. But it is common knowledge that corruption has not allowed such derivations from oil revenues to give meaningful dividends to the people. The Niger-Deltans who own the oil reserves desire more from the central government but the latter holds on to it. The fight for this resources birthed militancy, crude oil thefts and so many other problems. But then, elsewhere Gold deposit was discovered in Zamfara State in the North and then the people there insist the deposits belong to their State and not the federal government. The southern people definitely won't find it funny. A President of Northern origin shares their sentiment and sits on such bias and does nothing to quell the insult. That is the sort of economic conundrum that you get under a presidential system of government. Nepotism rather than federal character is at the gravest. We all know that this is not helpful in any way. Most of the unrest and insecurity that Nigeria witnessed over the last decade has an underlying power tussle for resource control, either sponsored by private entities or state actors. A more equitable system of resource control is needed to address these challenges.

Regional government could also help address some of the key political challenges in the country as well, including corruption, profligacy, and power imbalances. A decentralized system of government could promote greater accountability and transparency, and ensure that power is shared more evenly across the country.

Regional Governments Promote Efficient Resource Management

Because of various types of resources spread across different regions of Nigeria, resource control has been a major point of contention among the people. Regional government promotes efficient resource management by giving control of resources to the regions, which have a better understanding of their resources and can manage them better. This will ensure that resources are used effectively for the development of the regions.

One of the key benefits of regional governments is that it allows for the equitable distribution of resources. Resources are allocated to regions based on their needs, which ensures that every region receives the necessary resources to develop. Regional governments can also develop policies that are tailored to the specific needs of the region, which will lead to more effective management of resources.

Another benefit of regional government is that it promotes healthy competition between regions. Each region will strive to develop faster and better than others, which will lead to a faster rate of development across the country. Regional governments will also promote innovation and creativity as regions compete to attract investors and develop new industries.

Furthermore, regional governments promote accountability and transparency in the management of resources. Regional governments are closer to the people and are more accountable to them. This ensures that there is less corruption and mismanagement of resources, as the people can hold their leaders accountable.

Finally, regional governments can lead to better coordination and cooperation among regions. In a regional government system, regions can work together to achieve common goals and address common challenges. This will lead to more efficient resource management and faster development.

It is important to note that regional governments are not a panacea to all the problems facing Nigeria. However, it is clear that regional governments have the potential to promote more efficient resource management and faster development in the country.

Chapter 7

Benefits of Regional Government

A regional government has many benefits for Nigeria. It can lead to better governance by giving more power to the regions, allowing them to make decisions that are tailored to the needs of their communities. This can lead to better economic development as the regions can focus on developing their own resources, rather than waiting for the central government to do so. Additionally, a regional government can lead to political stability by reducing tensions between ethnic and religious groups, and allowing for greater cooperation between the regions and the central government. In this episode, we will explore these benefits in more detail.

Regional government offers several advantages over the current centralized system of government in Nigeria. First and foremost, it would promote better representation of the diverse ethnic and cultural groups in the country. Each region would have the power to determine its own development priorities, policies, and strategies, which would be more responsive to the needs of the people in the region. Another benefit of regional government is that it would encourage healthy competition among regions, thereby promoting innovation and development. Regions with abundant resources would be able to use them to attract investment and create jobs, while less-endowed regions would be encouraged to find creative solutions to their problems. Regional government would also lead to more efficient use of resources. Currently, many resources are wasted in the bureaucracy of the centralized system, and projects may be delayed or abandoned due to bureaucratic bottlenecks. Regional government would ensure that resources are used more efficiently, as decisions would be made closer to the people who are affected by them.

In addition, regional government would allow for greater accountability and transparency. Elected officials would be more accessible to their constituents, and citizens would have a greater say in the governance of their regions. This would make it more difficult for corrupt practices to take hold and lead to better governance.

The Benefits of Regional Government for Economic Development in Nigeria

As we have discussed in previous chapters, Nigeria is a diverse country with a vast array of economic potentials. However, our current centralized system of government has limited our ability to fully harness these potentials. A regional government system would give states more control over their economic resources, allowing them to make better use of their comparative advantages in various sectors in the sense that it would facilitate more collaboration between states within regions. States with similar economic strengths could create economic zones that allow for more intra-regional trade and investment. This would attract more foreign investment, create more jobs and boost economic growth.

A decentralized economic system would also lead to more accountability and transparency in the management of public resources. With states having more control over their resources, they would be more accountable for their use and better placed to ensure that these resources are used effectively to develop their regions.

Furthermore, the equitable distribution of resources and development across regions would reduce the perception of marginalization and ethnic tensions. This would ultimately promote social stability, national cohesion and economic growth.

The regions will be able to determine how best to allocate their resources and invest in their local economies, rather than being subject to the decisions of a central government. This will create more opportunities for economic growth and development, which will benefit both the regions and the country as a whole. Additionally, regional government will lead to more competition between the regions, which will drive innovation and improve efficiency. Each region will strive to attract investment and create a business-friendly environment in order to be competitive with other regions. This will lead to increased productivity and economic growth.

It is worth noting that some of the richest and most developed countries in the world, such as the United States and Germany, operate under a regional government system. So, as we continue to advocate for regional government in Nigeria, we must also consider the economic benefits that come with it.

Finally, regional government would promote national unity and cohesion by allowing each region to have a voice in the governance of the country. This would help to address the longstanding issues of marginalization and inequality that have plagued Nigeria for decades.

In conclusion, regional government offers several benefits over the current centralized system of government in Nigeria. It would promote better representation, healthy competition, efficient use of resources, greater accountability and transparency, and national unity and cohesion. It is time for Nigeria to seriously consider a shift towards regional government as a means of addressing the country's political and economic challenges.

Successful Regional Governments around the World

There are many examples of successful regional government systems around the world. For example, in India, regional governments have played a significant role in the country's economic development. In South Africa, regional governments have helped to address the country's historical injustices and promote reconciliation. Regional government played a significant role in South Africa's journey towards addressing historical injustices and promoting inclusivity. Following the end of apartheid in 1994, the country adopted a system of regional government, known as the provincial government system, which aimed to devolve power and resources to local communities.

One of the key benefits of regional government in South Africa was the promotion of diversity and inclusivity in politics. By giving more power to local communities, regional government allowed for greater representation of different ethnic and racial groups in decision-making processes. This helped to address the historical marginalization of certain groups, such as the black majority, who had been excluded from political power under apartheid.

In addition, regional government in South Africa has been instrumental in promoting economic development and reducing inequality. By devolving power and resources to local communities, regional government has allowed for more targeted and responsive economic development initiatives. For example, some of the most successful economic development initiatives in

South Africa, such as the Gauteng City Region and the Western Cape, have been driven by regional government.

Nigeria can learn from the South African example by adopting a similar approach to regional government. By devolving power and resources to local communities, Nigeria can promote inclusivity and diversity in politics, and drive economic development at the regional level.

One potential solution for Nigeria is to adopt a system of provincial governments, similar to that of South Africa. This would involve the creation of regional governments that have a significant degree of autonomy and decision-making power. These regional governments could be structured in a way that promotes diversity and inclusivity in politics, such as through the creation of reserved seats for minority groups.

Another potential solution is to empower local governments by devolving more power and resources to them. This would involve restructuring the current system of local government in Nigeria, which is currently highly centralized and controlled by the federal government. By giving more power to local governments, Nigeria can promote more responsive and targeted economic development initiatives, and ensure that local communities have a greater say in decision-making processes.

It is important to note that the success of regional government in South Africa was largely driven by political leadership and political will. As former South African President Nelson Mandela once stated, "It always seems impossible until it's done." Nigeria will need political leaders who are committed to driving the process of regional government implementation, and who are willing to work across ethnic and regional lines to promote inclusivity and diversity in politics.

Furthermore, civil society and the media will also play a critical role in promoting the idea of regional governments in Nigeria. By raising awareness about the benefits of regional government, and advocating for greater decentralization of power and resources, civil society and the media can help to build momentum for change.

In conclusion, South Africa's experience with regional government provides valuable lessons for Nigeria as it seeks to address its own political challenges. By adopting a similar approach to regional government, Nigeria can promote inclusivity and diversity in politics, drive economic development at the regional level, and reduce inequality. However, achieving this will require political leadership, political will, and the active involvement of civil society and the media.

Chapter 8

Regional Governments and National Unity

Nigeria has been plagued by ethnic and religious tensions that have undermined its political stability and economic development. These tensions have often been fuelled by a lack of inclusivity and representation in government, and a centralised system that favours certain regions over others. Regional governments offer a solution to this problem by creating more representative and inclusive political structures that can accommodate the diverse needs of Nigeria's many ethnic and religious groups. In this chapter, we will explore how regional governments can help to address the underlying factors driving ethnic and religious tensions in Nigeria, and promote diversity and inclusivity in Nigerian politics.

Impact of ethnic and religious tensions on Nigeria's political and economic development

Ethnic and religious tensions have had a profound impact on Nigeria's political and economic development. These tensions have led to violent conflicts and civil unrest, which have disrupted economic activity and led to the loss of many lives. The centralised nature of Nigeria's government has often exacerbated these tensions by creating a sense of exclusion and marginalisation among certain ethnic and religious groups. Regional governments can help to address these tensions by creating political structures that are more representative and inclusive.

Role of regional governments in promoting diversity and inclusivity in Nigerian politics

Regional governments can play a vital role in promoting diversity and inclusivity in Nigerian politics. By creating political structures that are more representative of the diverse needs of Nigeria's many ethnic and religious groups, regional governments can help to reduce feelings of exclusion and marginalisation. This, in turn, can help to reduce tensions and promote greater social cohesion. Countries such as the United States, Canada, and India have successfully implemented regional governments that promote diversity and inclusivity in their respective political systems.

Potential benefits of regional governments in promoting inter-ethnic and inter-religious dialogue and cooperation

Regional governments can also promote inter-ethnic and inter-religious dialogue and cooperation. By creating political structures that encourage cooperation and collaboration between different ethnic and religious groups, regional governments can help to build bridges and promote greater understanding and mutual respect. This can help to reduce tensions and promote social harmony. Countries such as Switzerland and Belgium have successfully implemented regional governments that promote inter-ethnic and inter-religious dialogue and cooperation.

Need for political leadership and political will to drive the process of regional government implementation

The successful implementation of regional governments in Nigeria will require strong political leadership and political will. Political leaders must be willing to embrace the idea of regional governments and push for constitutional amendments and restructuring to make it a reality. This will require a strong commitment to the idea of inclusivity and representation, and a willingness to confront the powerful interests that have benefited from Nigeria's centralised system of government.

Role of civil society and the media in promoting the idea of regional governments in Nigeria

Civil society and the media have a vital role to play in promoting the idea of regional governments in Nigeria. By educating the public on the benefits of regional governments and highlighting the flaws of Nigeria's current system, civil society and the media can help to build public support for regional governments. This can help to create pressure on political leaders to embrace the idea and push for its implementation. Countries such as South Africa and Kenya have successfully used civil society and the media to promote constitutional reforms and regional governments.

Regional governments offer a solution to Nigeria's long-standing ethnic and religious tensions. By creating more representative and inclusive political structures, regional governments can help to reduce feelings of exclusion and marginalisation and promote greater social cohesion. The successful implementation of regional governments in Nigeria will require strong political leadership, political will, and the support of civil society and the media. It is a long-term process, but the potential benefits of regional governments in promoting diversity, inclusivity, and inter-ethnic and inter-religious dialogue and cooperation make it a worthwhile endeavour.

"Debunking the Myths and Misconceptions of Regional Government"

There are some myths and misconceptions that surround regional government, I will try and explain why they are not true. Some people may believe that regional government would lead to more conflict and division among the different regions of Nigeria. Others may think that it would be too expensive or that it would lead to an imbalance in the distribution of resources. However, these beliefs are not necessarily true. Regional government can actually help to reduce conflict by giving each region more autonomy and allowing them to have more control over their own resources. It can also help to promote unity by allowing each region to have a say in the decisions that affect them.

Additionally, regional government can actually be more cost-effective than the current centralized system, as it can reduce bureaucracy and allow for more efficient decision-making. Furthermore, it can help to ensure a more equitable distribution of resources by allowing each region to have more control over their own resources.

In conclusion, regional government can offer many benefits to Nigeria and its people, and it is important to dispel any myths and misconceptions surrounding it.

Chapter 9

The Role of Non-Violent Agitation

As we come to the end of this book, it is important to reiterate that the demand for a regional government must be made using non-violent means. The youth of Nigeria have shown that they have the power to effect change in the country, but that power must be channelled in a peaceful and organized manner.

Non-violent means of protest have proven to be effective in the past. We can learn from the likes of Mahatma Gandhi and Martin Luther King Jr., who led successful non-violent movements for change. The key to a successful non-violent movement is organization and discipline. The youth of Nigeria must be organized and disciplined in their demand for a regional government. Non-violent agitation has played a significant role in advocating for political change in Nigeria before. From the struggle for independence to the fight against military rule, non-violent agitation has led to significant political change in the country. In advocating for a regional government, non-violent agitation can be a powerful tool for change. It allows citizens to express their views peacefully and effectively, and can galvanize support for the cause.

The #EndSARS protests in 2020 were largely peaceful and were able to bring attention to police brutality and demand for reforms. We must also recognize that violence only leads to more violence and can escalate quickly out of control. It is important to work towards a peaceful and non-violent solution to the political problems facing Nigeria.

There are several non-violent means of protest that can be used to demand for a regional government. These include peaceful demonstrations, sit-ins, boycotts, and strikes. These means of protest have been used successfully in the past and can be used again to demand for a regional system of government.

The agitation for regional government in Nigeria can be achieved through non-violent means. Non-violent means such as peaceful protests, lobbying and advocacy can be effective in persuading policymakers to implement regional government.

Non-violent means of agitation do not lead to the destruction of property and loss of lives, thus, ensuring social stability and order. The use of violence and forceful means to agitate for regional government would only lead to chaos, destruction of property, and loss of lives.

Non-violent means of agitation have been effective in achieving significant political and social changes in other countries, such as the Indian independence movement, the US civil rights movement and the fall of the apartheid regime in South Africa.

It is important to note that the demand for a regional government should not be limited to the youth alone. This is a demand that should be made by all Nigerians who believe in a better future for the country. It is a demand that should be made in a peaceful and organized manner.

Citizen participation is very important in governance. Regional government system has proven to be capable of increasing citizen participation by giving people more control over their local affairs. Citizen participation can promote transparency and accountability in governance. This system of government that prioritizes citizen participation is what is needed to solve the challenges of governance in Nigeria.

In conclusion, the youth of Nigeria have shown that they have the power to effect change in the country. The demand for a regional government is a just cause that must be made using non-violent means. This book is a call to action for the youth of Nigeria to sustain the energy they used in the #EndSARS and #Obidient movements and redirect it towards the demand for a regional system of government. Let us all join hands and demand for a better Nigeria.

Overcoming Resistance to Change

There is the potential for resistance to change which may arise in advocating for the constitutional restructuring of government in Nigeria. This must be expected because the established order will not likely permit a creative destruction that can throw them out of power and influence.

Change can be difficult, and there may be resistance to the idea of a regional government in Nigeria. Some may argue that a regional government will lead to further division and instability in the country. However, these arguments can be overcome through effective communication and engagement. By explaining the benefits of a regional government and addressing concerns, we can overcome resistance to change and build support for a new approach to governance in Nigeria.

Chapter 10

Call to Action

This book was published a week after 2023 Presidential election was won and winner declared. The date of release was intentional, just as the hash tagged title of the book. It didn't matter to me who'd win the presidential election before I set out to write this book because I believe the idea of constitutional restructuring has come. Frankly, no one can stop it, not even the politicians because the issue of self-determination has already even been crystallized within their ranks. The power play among all the country's political players in the tussle to ensure a southern president emerged in this election is a testament to that. What is needed now is for the idea to become catalysed by the voices and actions of all Nigerians. How fast this restructuring is achieved is now in the hands of all young people and citizens of this country.

There is no better time to ask for a regional government than now when the country has a southerner President-Elect. The demand for self-determination must begin from day one of the incoming government and young people will have a strong role to play in asking for this. In my opinion, it may be easier and with less collateral damage if this kind of demand is made under a Southerner President of Nigeria. The Northerners have not always shown any sign that they want to lay off their hold on the country considering the fact that most of the resources used in financing their budgets comes from oil proceeds from the south. The northern Nigeria would naturally be intolerant to constitutional restructuring and would not likely be disposed to a regional government because of their over-dependence on the southern region for economic reasons. It is not likely that a northerner president will ever allow self-determination, at least not easily. You can see the harsh treatment and experiences of agitators of Biafra and Yoruba nation under the Buhari-led government. Even though the approach from these agitators has been violent in many cases which necessitated a show of force from the government in retroaction, the Buhari-led government hardly gave the agitators a table to talk about their interests. Self-determination is a right and no part of the country must be denied to express their interests in the regard. So, Nigeria cannot afford any brutal or violent self-determination process and that is why I believe under a southerner president, there could be room for referendum without any brutal resistance from the presidency or its collateral apparatus. This is a chance that Nigerians must take and an opportunity they must seize in getting the country restructured and repositioned for the true definition of 'unity in diversity'.

The #EndSARS and #Obidient movements have proven that young people in Nigeria have the power to effect change in the country. They have shown resilience, tenacity, and bravery in the face of oppression and injustice. The movements have inspired hope and demonstrated that young people can no longer be ignored in the political sphere. However, to truly create a lasting impact, we must redirect this energy towards the demand for regional government in Nigeria.

The instrument of the social media is still a potent one to begin the #RegionalGovt conversation and then go on to organise with civil society organizations, and all relevant stakeholders in the country. The mainstream politicians tried to downplay social media influence on Nigeria's recent elections but clearly they have been proven wrong by the numbers. Social media is a strong structure of young people, where the decision of future Nigeria is going to be made. No politician is ever going to undermine young people anymore because they have found their voices, the only one thing that has been taken away from them for a long time. The internet has given back voices to citizens all over the world, any government that fails to listen and act does that to its own peril. If there are any people who know how to use their voices, it is Nigerians, the most populous Black Country in the World. There is no better time to use this voice than now.

The people must act now. Young people must sustain the momentum of the #EndSARS and #Obidient movements and channel it towards the demand for regional government. This demand must be made clear to parliamentary representatives from different parts of the country and their work in the regard should form their score card for re-election. This demand must be made in a peaceful and non-violent manner, using all available democratic means. We must engage with our representatives, participate in the electoral process, and hold those in power accountable for their actions.

We must also work towards creating a united front of young people across the country. We must bridge the divides that exist between regions, religions, and ethnic groups and come together under a common cause. This will require dialogue, understanding, and a commitment to creating a better Nigeria for all.

As we have seen throughout this book, a regional system of government would address many of the issues that the country is faced with. It would bring government closer to the people, allowing for better representation and accountability. It would also foster healthy competition between regions, leading to greater development and progress. Moreover, a regional system would promote cultural diversity and preserve the unique identities of each region.

The road to regional government in Nigeria is a long and arduous one, but it is a journey worth embarking on. By working together towards a common goal, we can create a government that is accountable, transparent, and responsive to the needs of its people.

We have seen the benefits of regional government in other countries, and we can achieve similar success in Nigeria. The task ahead requires sustained advocacy and political will to overcome resistance and change the status quo.

Let us not be discouraged by the challenges we may encounter along the way, but rather let us be motivated by the possibilities of a better future for our country. We must continue to engage with policymakers, elected officials, civil society organizations, and other stakeholders to build support for regional government in Nigeria. Through sustained advocacy and non-violent means, we can make regional government a reality and transform Nigeria's political landscape for the better.

Let me remind you again that a regional government can be a solution to Nigeria's political challenges. It can promote economic development, political stability, accountability, transparency, and citizen participation in governance. By exploring examples from other countries and using non-violent agitation, we can build support for a regional government and overcome resistance to change. It is time for Nigeria to consider a new approach to governance, one that is tailored to the needs of its diverse communities. Let us work towards a regional government that will bring about positive change for the country and its citizens.

Finally, we must be patient and persistent. The fight for regional government will not be easy, and we may face setbacks and challenges along the way. But we must not give up. We must continue to advocate for change and work towards a better future for ourselves and for generations to come.

In closing, the demand for regional government is not just a political issue, but a moral imperative. It is our duty as young people to demand a system of government that works for us and for all Nigerians. We have the power to effect change, and we must use it wisely and responsibly. Let us continue to raise our voices and demand for a better Nigeria, where regional government exists to promote peace, justice, and progress.

Addendum

Implementing Regional Government in Nigeria

Implementing regional government in Nigeria will require constitutional amendments and a restructuring of the country. The first step towards implementing regional government is to amend the constitution to devolve power to the states of the federation. There had been calls for state police over the years but the federal government under the hands of successive presidents have been reluctant to allow the restructuring of the police. The first step towards achieving this goal is to initiate a constitutional review process that will lead to the necessary amendments to the constitution. The process should be transparent, participatory and inclusive, with all stakeholders including civil society groups, traditional rulers, political parties, and the public at large being involved.

Public Education and Awareness:

One of the major challenges facing the implementation of regional government is the lack of public awareness and understanding of the concept. Therefore, it is important to carry out a sustained public education and awareness campaign to sensitize the public on the benefits of regional government, the restructuring of the police, and other key issues that will arise during the implementation process. This book sets to achieve the objectives of educating Nigerians in these areas.

Building Consensus among Key Stakeholders

Implementing regional government in Nigeria will require the buy-in of key stakeholders, including political elites, traditional rulers, civil society groups, and the public at large. Therefore, it is important to build consensus among these groups by engaging in dialogue, consultation and negotiation to address any concerns and ensure that everyone is on board.

Adequate Funding

Adequate funding will be required to ensure the smooth implementation of regional government. The federal government will need to provide the necessary financial resources to support the establishment of new regional structures and institutions, as well as to facilitate the transfer of power and resources from the federal to the regional governments.

Strengthening of Institutions

The successful implementation of regional government will require the strengthening of key institutions such as the judiciary, civil service, and the police. The regional governments will need to establish their own independent judiciary systems and invest in training and development of the civil service and police to ensure that they have the capacity to function effectively in the new system.

In summary, implementing regional government in Nigeria will require constitutional amendments, public education and awareness, building consensus among key stakeholders, adequate funding, and the strengthening of institutions. These steps will be crucial to ensure the success of regional government in Nigeria and will require a sustained effort and commitment from all stakeholders involved.

ABOUT THE AUTHOR

Victor Alade is a Nigerian-born author, political commentator, public policy analyst, and human rights investigator. Born on October 1st, 1985 in Iyin Ekiti, a small town in Nigeria, Victor has always been passionate about advocating for responsible leadership in government and politics.

He holds a Master's degree and has spent years investigating human rights abuses in Nigeria, with a focus on advocating for justice for victims of civil and political rights violations like police brutality and extra-judicial killings. As a political commentator and public policy analyst, Victor Alade brings a unique perspective to the table, offering insights that are as relevant as they are timely.

Aside from his writing and public speaking engagements, Victor is also the founder of the Victor Alade Foundation for Integrity Development (VFID), a non-governmental organization that focuses on integrity education and anti-corruption awareness for young people. He is also the Anticorruption Initiative Assessment lead for public and private institutions. Through the work of his organization, he has been instrumental in driving the conversation around the need for ethical leadership and the eradication of corruption in public and private institutions.

Married with two kids, a son, and a daughter, Victor's latest book, "From #EndSARS to #RegionalGovt: *The Youth-Led Movement for Change*," is a testament to his passion for positive change in Nigeria.

Victor's dedication to improving the lives of others is exemplified in his decision to donate 30% of the book's sales profit to widows above 60 years and orphans in his hometown. He believes that the book's message can bring about positive change in Nigeria and beyond.

"From #EndSARS to #RegionalGovt: The Youth-Led Movement for Change" is not just a book for Victor, but it is a call to action for all young people in Nigeria and beyond.

www.ingramcontent.com/pod-product-compliance
Lightning Source LLC
LaVergne TN
LVHW050320160826
845677LV00014B/3496

* 9 7 8 9 7 8 5 8 9 4 0 2 8 *